UP THREE POINTS, PLEASE

"Try to picture it after you've poured 20 thousand into it."

UP THREE POINTS, PLEASE

Cartoons from
THE WALL STREET JOURNAL
Selected by Charles Preston

TRIDENT PRESS / NEW YORK

SBN: 671-27067-2.

Library of Congress Catalog Card Number: 75–126628

Published simultaneously in the United States and
Canada by Trident Press, a division of Simon & Schuster,
Inc., 630 Fifth Avenue, New York, N.Y. 10020

PRINTED IN THE UNITED STATES OF AMERICA

UP THREE POINTS, PLEASE

Up and down, up and down . . . it's hard to decide who to feel more sorry for, the harried businessman or the elevator operator!

We've found that the successful businessman usually has a reserve of humor to carry him through the "downs" and keep his head from swelling during the "ups." We've also found that the successful businessman is usually a regular reader of *The Wall Street Journal*.

We know he's responsive to the news we report and to the advertising we carry. He responds to our cartoons too, so we've collected them in this book.

Enjoy. May all your stocks go up three points this very day.

THE WALL STREET JOURNAL

"Miss Pettifog, take a crank letter."

"When you're making plans for this evening, Harvey, just
remember I'm tax-deductible."

"If you could live your life all over again, what stocks would
you buy?"

"For heaven's sake, Walter. Can board chairmen have measles?"

"Thanks just the same, Charley, but I can't afford another
tip on the market."

"Get down to Brownell, Brownell, Durston, and Fisk, Harvey, and do your thing."

"We've got the apple, peach, and cherry market sewed up, girls. I say it's high time we went after a piece of the gooseberry action."

"The establishment awaits."

"Sir, are you in?"

"Can we afford anything yet?"

"Ooh. . . It's just beautiful!"

"Since I convinced myself it's only a game, there's no fun in it."

"Say, sonny, you really want to protest something—sing about the rise in the consumer price index!"

"But tell me *why* you want to move back to the suburbs after we just fled the suburbs where we had originally moved to get out of the city."

"You probably don't remember us, but I used to recite poetry and
Marge played the dulcimer here back in '58–'59. . ."

"Look, Mr. Prescott doesn't even see *me*!"

"And I would like to remind you good people that the cost of
salvation has gone up too."

"I see it as a poetic statement of the alienation of man in our times.
George sees it as a hedge against inflation."

"No, you can't do it over."

"Please tell me it's Sunday."

"Sometimes I think these Christmas gratuities are getting out
of hand."

"Sometimes I think about the sun burning out in a few billion years or an intergalactic collision and I wonder: 'What's the use?'"

"What kind of Christmas would it be if we only spent what
you could afford?"

"At first we thought Timmy was an underachiever. Then we
thought it might be some type of cultural denial. Our
current thinking is that he just isn't bright."

"Doesn't it count for anything that your father's been making the scene more than twice as long as you've been making the scene?"

"Harold, if we don't turn on now, we probably *never* will!"

"The kingdom is secure, sire—we have developed an
anti-arrow arrow!"

"When I get out I think I'll go legit. You know, pornography or something."

"I just sold my birthright for two shares of IBM."

"I still can't get over it. Me, a poor immigrant boy, achieving all
this by marrying the boss's daughter."

"We are agreed, then, 40% precipitation probability?"

"Relax! It's on automatic pilot."

"Gracious, I don't want to bring him back. I'd just like his
advice on some investments."

"I'm just showing her
what she'll have to
put up with while I'm gone."

"I don't have to tell you where
I'm running away to until you let
me talk to a lawyer."

"Every Monday it's the same thing with you. But you're always
on that 8:13 bus!"

"Remember when it meant cents instead of dollars?"

"This is the worst piece of garbage I've ever had the pleasure of publishing!"

"You are neat, courteous, industrious, reliable and considerate.
Your days are numbered."

"Got everything—books, lunch, bail money?"

"I know just what you mean. While you were circling up there waiting to land, I was driving around and around down here looking for a place to park."

"I just put a pin in a place where nobody will ever think of
looking for one!"

"How come you don't feel alienated when your mother makes
chocolate whipped cream cake?"

"I just said 'Thank you' to a recording!"

"It's bad enough he's asleep on the job but he belongs with the company across the hall."

"Sorry we couldn't do business but you'll have to admit, we had a good laugh."

"It's delicious—how much is the franchise?"

"You'd better take me out. This is the wrong day for a Sagittarius
and the bases loaded."

"It might be better if you didn't refer to my parents as the
'white power structure.' "

"I said I'd name it after her."

"The truth of the matter, Joanie, I really enjoy the middle class values."

"I already gave at the IRS office."

"Flight 304 requests permission to land—
they've been circling for the last
3 days and they're running out of food."

"We had a riot in our class, so we got out early."

"Does it seem to you air pollution is getting more and more
concentrated lately?"

"Oh gosh, yes! We sell them faster than we can call them back!"

"Lots of men wear shorts in the summertime!"

"They're just resting between movements.
There isn't *supposed* to
be a commercial."

"Up three points, please."

"Junior has asked me to ask you to please stop saying 'cool' and
'groovy' when he brings his friends around."

"It's my own plan for making automobiles safe!"

"I'm sorry, sir, but according
to our computer you do not exist."

"I'll unpack later. I'm writing home for money."

"... And this is either my son John or my daughter Janie."

"You've said it all, Myron."

"There's no point in going there all the time if nobody
believes in you!"

"How could Daddy have the heart to order me to my room
when it's such a mess?"

"No, no, honey. Little *girls* wear lockets. Little boys wear *beads.*"

"They're not praying—one of them lost a contact lens."

"Does the gentleman have an appointment?"

"Thanks for the order, J.R.
Now how about another eighteen . . .
this time for *real*?"

"I'm sorry but Mr. Dewlap is out of town. . . No, Mr. Clement is
in Europe. . . Mr. Fallon is in Boston. . . Mr. Preston's gone for
the day. . . No, Mr. Herrod is on vacation. Good Heavens! I'm
the only one here!"

". . . . Dewlap. . . . Shorthand. . . . Institute. . . . Gentlemen. . . .
colon. . . . your. . . . course. . . . of. . . . instruction. . . .
apparently. . . . leaves. . . . a. . . . lot. . . . to. . . .
be. . . . desired. . . ."

"Never mind, Dad, I'll walk to Sunday school."

"Hey, kid—I want to talk to you."

"How do I deal with a patron who is overdrawn and is full of remorse and she's in tears?"

"Let's see, now. Two eggs separated . . ."

"I had a man-to-man talk with my boy about the facts of life,
Doctor. I'd like to check on a number of things he told me."

1.

2.

"What eats me is the 70 grand
I hid in '39 ain't worth
half of that now!"

"Look at it this way, sir—you're in your second
childhood only once."

"How come you never bring any salt home from the mines?"

"I'll say one thing for it—at last I've seen a purple cow!"

"I still liked it better when you were vice-president of marketing
for the Acme Corporation."

"See anything of a pair of lost glasses on your way
down here, ma'am?"

"What we want on this TV special is an accurate account of the
situation currently confronting mankind that pulls no punches but
at the same time doesn't interfere with the viewer's will to
consume homemade frozen dinners."

"Good-by upper middle class. Hello, lower upper."

"This steak is burned—just what kind of an airline is this, anyhow?"

"But if we let *one* car on the sidewalk, we'll have to let *all* cars on the sidewalk."

"Perkins, my son is joining the firm. Keep him out of sight."

"Who's Betty?"

"They're basically a sound corporation—with a lousy taste for art!"

"Is there anything bothering you, Purvis? We notice you spend a lot of time staring out of the window."

"Can I have the car keys? I missed the school bus!"

"That's the hole Ralph made in one."

"Let's not get upset about it, Chauncey. It's not
against you personally."

"Get more fresh air. Stay indoors . . ."

"There's a movie I want to see. Come on, keep swallowing!"

"I believe in planned parenthood . . . wish I could
have planned mine."

"What did we ever do with our evenings, Henry, before
we became aware?"

"One curds and whey."

"I came in early. I wanted to see you in action."

"But, Tom, if we eliminate government corruption, racial violence, and crime in the streets, I shudder to think what will move into the vacuum!"

"It's a fine time to tell me you're allergic to wool."

"I only agreed to take care of their dog because I thought they
were going *away* on their vacation!"

"My old man said if I burned my draft card, he would burn
his check book!"

"As president of State, I wish you all the best of luck; especially the
66⅔% of you who will drop out after midterms."

"Yes, the doctor will consider a house call—what time can you
be at his house?"

"Suppose I toss you a few symptoms and you take it from there."

"Seriously, don't you think this is better than accepting
a Federal handout?"

"Play money or not, Wilkins, I told you to cut that out!"

"Just how do I relate to all this stuff, Miss Jones?"

"I'm starved. All I had to eat was a few olives."

"The way I see it, those of us in the 95% bracket constitute a
minority group, and we have *our* rights, too."

"Can't you finish your studies in business administration and then
relate to humanity on the side or something?"

"It's as safe as a car can be, before some nut gets behind the wheel."

"Our trip to Philadelphia was marvelous! The airport was socked
in and we had to land in San Francisco!"

"On the other hand, Mr. Holmes, having a negative personality is better than having no personality at all!"

"The file system is a secret handed down from secretary to secretary."

"My account number is 29-732-5, but I can't remember my name."

"Following the morning devotions, we'll adjourn to the recreation room for a groovy poetry reading and folk sing-in sponsored by the young moderns' class."

"Ten *more* commandments?"

"I better hang up, honey. I think someone wants to use the phone."

"If I stopped at every sign that said 'Stop' I'd never get anywhere."

"Well, the worst part of the day is over . . . getting here!"

"Now may I have a glass of water?"

"That's not the way my father used to cook them."

"Moving back to the city—please be kind to our arborvitae."

"I'll need a bigger allowance, Dad. I'm getting married."

"If you want a winning football team there's only one way
to do it . . . de-emphasize education!"

"When the newness wears off, will you park it in the garage?"

"The time is coming, it says here, when you can go day after day
without cash. How about that?"

"For heaven's sake, Morton. What the American Bar Association
doesn't know won't hurt them."

"Just for openers, get me one share of each."

"Yes, madam, we make house calls."

"... and never worry about losing your identity around here!
You'll always be good old 6400-97-80112 to us!"

"Establishment written all over him!"

"Well, one day I sent away for one of those crazy
get-rich-quick schemes."

"From your books I pictured you as a dirty old man."

"You mean for 23 years *your* work has consisted of
checking *my* work?"

"Mr. Barton wants to see you in his office immediately, Mr. Moore.
I think it's important."

"So what if you *are* a sight? Heck, I see gussied-up dolls all day long!"

"George, I think I'm confused. Are we the WASPs or the Honkies, or both?"

"I suppose it was inevitable!"

"I know you can do this in your sleep—but must you?"

"Without going into the financial details—we have to return to
'Go' and start over."

"He says he'll hold the phone while I ask if you're in."

"I certainly didn't come all the way over here to listen to
'Short'nin' Bread'!"

"It has counted our blessings. There were 384,259 of them, to be exact."

"Burke and Company will just have to adjust, Ed. I'm letting the sideboards *grow*."

"Never mind all that price ratio data—just plug me into the action!"

"I'm broke. Isn't that reason enough?"

"I had the same thing for lunch."

"He may cry a little. It's his first haircut."

"I've *got* to make it to work—I can't use up my
sick leave being sick!"

"How tastes change! Three years ago this shocked the
Cannes Film Festival."

"It's your baby sitter—she wants to know how much liability
insurance you have."

"Your mother and I can't begin to tell you how nice it is to have you home for the holidays."

"Well, there was this chick named Alice. And, man, like she was grooving on this beautiful high . . ."

"President Truman? What's he doing in U.S. history?"

"I never thought it would end like this."